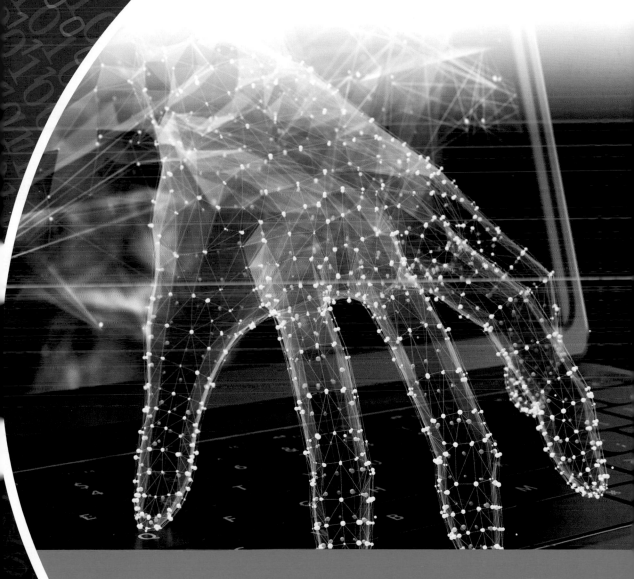

PRIVACY IN
THE DIGITAL AGE

CYBERCRIME

BY HEATHER C. HUDAK

CONTENT CONSULTANT
M. E. Kabay, PhD, CISSP-ISSMP
Professor of Computer Information Systems
Norwich University

Core Library

An Imprint of Abdo Publishing
abdobooks.com

Cover image: Cybercrime often involves theft and
invasion of privacy.

abdocorelibrary.com

Published by Abdo Publishing, a division of ABDO, PO Box 398166, Minneapolis, Minnesota 55439. Copyright © 2020 by Abdo Consulting Group, Inc. International copyrights reserved in all countries. No part of this book may be reproduced in any form without written permission from the publisher. Core Library™ is a trademark and logo of Abdo Publishing.

Printed in the United States of America, North Mankato, Minnesota
032019
092019

 THIS BOOK CONTAINS RECYCLED MATERIALS

Cover Photo: iStockphoto
Interior Photos: iStockphoto, 1; Sean Pavone/Shutterstock Images, 4–5; Especial/Notimex/Newscom, 7; Red Line Editorial, 9, 41; ESB Professional/Shutterstock Images, 12–13; Jerry Cleveland/The Denver Post/Getty Images, 15; Kyodo/AP Images, 18–19, 45; Sal Veder/AP Images, 21; John Hayes/AP Images, 24; Olivier Douliery/Abaca Press/Sipa USA/AP Images, 26–27; Oliver Contreras/Sipa USA/AP Images, 29, 43; Frank Augstein/AP Images, 31; David Paul Morris/Bloomberg/Getty Images, 34–35; Shutterstock Images, 38

Editor: Maddie Spalding
Series Designer: Megan Ellis

Library of Congress Control Number: 2018966068

Publisher's Cataloging-in-Publication Data

Names: Hudak, Heather C., author.
Title: Cybercrime / by Heather C. Hudak
Description: Minneapolis, Minnesota: Abdo Publishing, 2020 | Series: Privacy in the digital age | Includes online resources and index.
Identifiers: ISBN 9781532118906 (lib. bdg.) | ISBN 9781532173080 (ebook) | ISBN 9781644940815 (pbk.)
Subjects: LCSH: Cybercrimes--Juvenile literature. | World Wide Web--Security measures--Juvenile literature. | Computer crimes--United States--Prevention--Juvenile literature. | Privacy, Right of--United States--Juvenile literature.
Classification: DDC 005.8--dc23

CONTENTS

CHAPTER
ONE

SHUTTING DOWN A CITY

Atlanta, Georgia, is one of the largest cities in the United States. It is home to nearly 6 million people. Many large companies have headquarters in Atlanta. So when hackers took over the city's computer systems on March 22, 2018, the ripple effect was felt far and wide.

On the morning of the attack, city workers knew immediately that something was wrong. Some of the icons on their computer desktops had been replaced with black boxes. Files had been renamed "weapologize" or "imsorry." More than one-third of the city's software

Atlanta, Georgia, is a bustling city.

TYPES OF HACKERS

A hacker is someone who breaks into computer systems. Hackers who use their skills for personal gain are called black-hat hackers. Other hackers help solve problems or protect against the work of black-hat hackers. They are called white-hat hackers. They get permission before they break into systems. Grey-hat hackers break into systems without the system owner's permission. But they do not do any damage. They explore ways to improve the system. Some unskilled hackers are called script kiddies. They know very little about computers. They use tools called scripts that other hackers have created to break into systems.

programs were under cyberattack. Many programs were linked to critical services. Courts had to cancel hearings. People could not pay their bills online.

Hackers used ransomware to take control of the city's computer network. Ransomware is a type of software. It encrypts files. Encryption makes data unreadable. The data can only be decrypted, or made readable again, with a piece of software called

Ransomware gives users a countdown to when their files will be lost.

a decryption key. The hackers promised to provide a decryption key if the city paid them $51,000. The city did not pay the hackers. It had to replace damaged devices and upgrade software. This cost the city millions of dollars. It took weeks for businesses to return to normal. A large amount of data was lost forever. This data included legal documents and police recordings. Law enforcement began to look into how the attack took place. City officials learned that they should have made copies of their data and software. They should have kept those copies separate from their main computer system. Then they would not have lost so much data.

TOOLS OF THE TRADE

Hackers can break into computer systems in many different ways. Many hackers use a type of software called malware. Malware is designed to damage or destroy computers and computer systems. It is often disguised as a game or an app.

Ransomware is a type of malware. Other common types of malware are viruses, worms, and Trojan horses. Viruses are programs or computer code that damage computers. A virus latches onto a normal program, file, or document. It makes copies of itself. Then it spreads to other computers in the same network. Worms also make copies of themselves. They spread from one computer network to another through weaknesses in the network, such as a software bug. Trojan horses are programs that appear to be harmless. They may claim to protect a user's device from viruses. But when the user downloads the program, it infects the user's computer with a virus.

CYBERCRIME COMPLAINTS

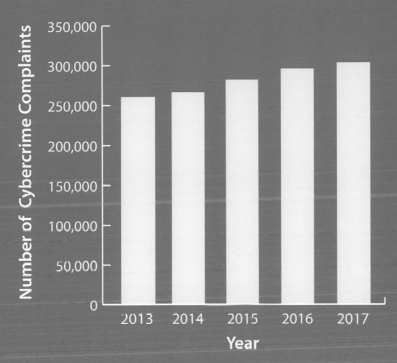

The Internet Crime Complaint Center monitors the number of cybercrime complaints each year. This center is run by the Federal Bureau of Investigation (FBI). The above graph shows the number of cybercrime complaints in the United States from 2013 to 2017. What trend do you notice? What do you think may be some reasons for this trend?

Another strategy some cybercriminals use is a denial-of-service (DoS) attack. This type of attack involves sending thousands of messages to a computer system at once. The system cannot keep up with all this information. It slows down or stops working. This prevents people from using the network.

SMART CITIES

Atlanta is a smart city. Smart cities use technology to improve the services they provide. For example, many smart cities use sensors to control traffic lights and other objects. Smart cities provide residents with a better quality of life. But they are also more likely to face cyberattacks. This is because they rely on computers and other digital technologies. Some people think smart cities are not doing enough to protect against cyberattacks. They think smart cities need to work more closely with cybersecurity experts. Experts can help educate cities on ways to better protect themselves.

CYBERATTACKS

Experts believe hackers earned more than $1 billion in ransomware attacks in 2016. In May 2017, North Korean hackers used ransomware to attack more than 150 countries. They shut down health-care systems in the United Kingdom. They broke into computer networks in Russia. Similar attacks are becoming more common every day.

STRAIGHT TO THE
SOURCE

Cesar Cerrudo helps protect computer systems from cyberattacks. In a 2018 interview, he said:

> It [the Atlanta cyberattack] could have been a lot worse. Last year Dallas's alarm system was hacked, and tornado sirens were fired at night for one or two hours until the authorities could turn them off. That resulted in panic and 4,000 calls to 911. In 2016, San Francisco's railway system was also hit by ransomware, so they had to let the people ride for free until they could recover the system. . . .
>
> In the case of Atlanta, it doesn't seem like critical systems were affected. The cyber criminals just wanted to do the least effort to get the maximum profit. . . . So I think it was, you know, luck. If a serious attacker proposed to bring down a city, they could do it.

Source: Linda Poon. "Why Are Cities So Vulnerable to Cyber Attack?" *CityLab*. CityLab, March 30, 2018. Web. Accessed December 12, 2018.

Back It Up

The author of this passage is using evidence to support a point. Write a paragraph describing the point the author is making. Then write down two or three pieces of evidence the author uses to make the point.

CHAPTER
TWO

COMMON CYBERCRIMES

There are many types of cybercrimes. Some cybercrimes affect many people. Hackers may damage computers or computer networks. They can destroy data and take computers offline. Other cybercrimes target individual people. Some hackers commit identity theft. They gain access to data without permission. This data can include personal information, such as credit card numbers. Personal data is part of a person's identity. Hackers use this data to pretend to be someone else. They may steal people's

Some hackers steal personal data, such as credit card information.

identities for personal gain. For example, they may use stolen credit card numbers to buy things.

CYBERBULLYING

Nearly 2.5 billion people worldwide have at least one social media account. Facebook, Twitter, and Instagram are popular social media sites. Some cybercriminals search social media sites for private information about people. They use this information to guess people's passwords and break into their accounts. Some cybercriminals send or post hurtful messages to people on social media. This crime is called cyberbullying.

ONLINE HARASSMENT

Cyberbullying occurs when people threaten or harass others online. Some cyberbullies know their victims. They target a person for a reason. Other bullies choose random victims. Often the messages they send are anonymous. The victim does not know who the bully is. Cyberstalking is a form of cyberbullying. Cyberstalkers spy on people and invade their privacy. They may harass people and try to make them fear for their safety.

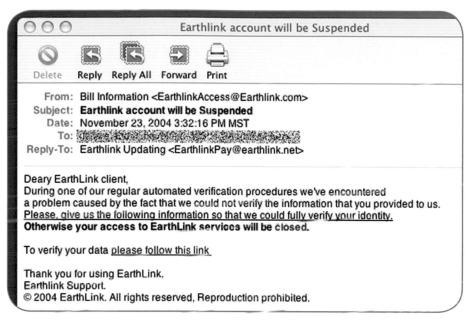

Phishing emails are designed to alarm people into taking action.

The purpose of cyberbullying is to cause distress or make people feel bad about themselves.

SCAMS

Many hackers try to trick people into sharing their private data. One common method hackers use is phishing. They send emails or texts that appear to be from a company the person trusts, such as a bank. The messages contain a link. In some cases, clicking on the link uploads malware onto the person's device.

In other cases, the link may take a person to a website. The site is designed to look official. It asks the person to fill in personal information. The hacker uses this information to break into the person's accounts.

In September 2018, the Federal Bureau of Investigation (FBI) warned of a kidnapping scam. Cybercriminals sent messages to people through social media and texts. The messages told people to call a phone number. When people called this number, they heard a woman screaming for help. The cybercriminals tried to convince people that they had kidnapped a friend or family member. The cybercriminals told people to send them money or the person would be killed.

The cybercriminals had to act fast before word of the scam spread. The easiest way to check whether such calls are real is to call the person who is declared to be in danger. But the victims of the scam were not given much time to contact police or their family before the deadline to pay was up.

EXPLORE ONLINE

Chapter Two talks about different types of cybercrimes. The article at the website below goes into more depth on this topic. How is the information from the website the same as the information in Chapter Two? What new information did you learn from the website?

THE INTERNET AND CRIME
abdocorelibrary.com/cybercrime

A HISTORY OF HACKING

The word *hacking* often has a negative meaning. But this was not always the case. At one time, hacking was a fun way for people to solve problems or show off their computer skills. The first computer hackers were students at the Massachusetts Institute of Technology (MIT) in the 1960s. They explored and improved computer systems. Some of these hackers helped develop the Advanced Research Projects Agency Network (ARPANET). The ARPANET was the basis for the modern internet.

Each year at the DEF CON conference in Las Vegas, Nevada, people from all over the world learn about hacking.

THE ARPANET

In the 1960s, a government agency called the Advanced Research Projects Agency (ARPA) was exploring ways to connect computers. It developed a computer network called the Advanced Research Projects Agency Network (ARPANET). In 1969 researchers used ARPANET to connect a computer at the University of California, Los Angeles to a computer at Stanford Research Institute near San Francisco. The world's first email message was sent between these computers. Researchers then connected computers at other universities to the same network. The modern internet grew from the ARPANET.

PHREAKERS

It was not long before some people discovered other ways to use their hacking skills. In the 1970s, some people began hacking into phone systems. These people were called phone hackers, or phreakers. They wanted to make free long-distance calls. John Draper was one of the first and most well-known phreakers. His scheme involved a toy whistle from a cereal box. The sound that triggered the phone system to make a long-distance call was high-pitched. The toy

Steve Jobs, *left*, and Steve Wozniak, *right*, were phreakers before they founded Apple in 1976.

whistle made a similar sound. Draper used the whistle to hack into telephone networks. He was arrested several times for fraud. Other famous phreakers include Steve Jobs and Steve Wozniak. Jobs and Wozniak founded the technology company Apple.

MAKING HEADLINES

By the early 1980s, the word *hacking* began to take on a new meaning. It was used to talk about computer experts who were up to no good. A movie about hacking called *WarGames* inspired a group of teenage hackers. The hackers were from Milwaukee, Wisconsin. Milwaukee's area code is 414. The hackers called themselves the 414s. They hacked into the computer systems of dozens of organizations.

The FBI found out about the 414s when the hackers accidentally deleted files in a system they hacked. At the time, there were no laws against hacking. This incident spurred lawmakers to create six bills to protect people from computer crimes. One of these bills became the Computer Fraud and Abuse Act. This act was passed in 1984. It made using a computer without permission a federal crime. The punishment for breaking this law is up to five years in prison and a fine of up to $250,000 for the first offense. The prison time and fine are greater for later offenses.

THE INTERNET

The internet became popular in the 1990s. It created new opportunities for hackers. People could connect to computer systems all over the world. There were often bugs in these systems. Many people did not know how to protect themselves from cyberattacks.

Cybercrimes became more common in the 1990s. In 1999 a computer virus infected one-fifth of all the world's computers.

PERSPECTIVES
KEVIN MITNICK

Kevin Mitnick is a hacker and cybersecurity expert. He was on the FBI's Most Wanted list of criminals in the mid-1990s. He had hacked into more than 40 major companies. He stole software and data. He damaged computer systems. In 1995 he was arrested for stealing 20,000 credit cards. He spent nearly five years in jail. After his release, the US government asked him to help solve a computer crime. Today, Mitnick helps protect organizations from cyberattacks. He also gives speeches about cybersecurity. He says, "The purpose of my public speaking is to raise awareness."

Kevin Mitnick was a well-known hacker in the 1990s.

It was called the Melissa virus. This was the first worldwide computer virus outbreak. It gave the world a glimpse of what was to come. In the early 2000s, many large companies were hit by DoS attacks. These companies included Yahoo, eBay, and Amazon.

THE COST OF CYBERATTACKS

Each year, there are approximately 800,000 cyberattacks on computer and internet users. In September 2018, US authorities arrested a man who was part of a Russian hacking gang. The gang had hacked into several major US financial companies. Between 2012 and 2015, gang members stole the personal data of more than 100 million Americans. They used people's credit card information to make purchases and withdraw money. It was one of the biggest financial hacks to date. Experts believe cybercrimes such as these will cost the world $6 trillion a year by 2021.

FURTHER EVIDENCE

Chapter Three explores the history of hacking. What was one of the main points of this chapter? What key evidence supports this point? Read the article at the website below. Does the information on the website support this point? Or does it present new evidence?

A BRIEF HISTORY OF HACKING
abdocorelibrary.com/cybercrime

A GROWING THREAT

Cybercrime is the fastest-growing type of crime in the United States. It is the biggest threat facing businesses around the world. Anyone can be the victim of a cybercrime.

In 2013 hackers attacked 3 billion accounts on the website Yahoo. They gained access to people's usernames, birthdates, and passwords. This was the largest-known security breach to date. Four years later, hackers broke into Equifax's computer system. Equifax is one of the biggest credit reporting agencies in the United States. Credit reporting agencies keep

The former chief executive officer of Equifax testified before the US House of Representatives in 2017 after a data breach exposed people's data.

track of people's payment histories. They find out how good a person is at managing debt. These agencies collect a lot of data from people. The Equifax security breach exposed the data of more than 143 million people. Hackers could use this data to commit identity theft.

PERSPECTIVES
CYBERSECURITY

Maya Horowitz is a cybersecurity expert. She helps protect computer systems from threats. She believes it is important to update software and systems often. This will help limit the impact of cyberattacks such as WannaCry. Horowitz said, "The greatest lesson [of the WannaCry scam] is that each and every one of us is a target for cyber tools and weapons."

WANNACRY

In 2017 hackers launched a huge ransomware attack. They used a bug in the Microsoft Windows operating system to infect computers with ransomware. The ransomware was called WannaCry. It quickly spread around the world. It encrypted files. It demanded $300 in Bitcoin from each computer user. Bitcoin is

White House officials gave a briefing about the WannaCry attack and the countries it affected in 2017.

an electronic currency. Hackers would only send a decryption key after the payment was made.

Microsoft knew about the bug in its operating system. The company released a patch one month before the attacks. A patch is a change to a program that is meant to fix or update it. But many people

BITCOIN

Bitcoin is a type of digital money. An unknown person created it in 2009. The money is not kept in a bank. It only exists online. Government or financial institutions do not control the money. Bitcoin owners are anonymous. They have a private address that they can use to send and receive Bitcoins through the internet. Many cybercriminals ask for ransom in Bitcoins. This allows them keep their identities secret.

did not update their Windows operating systems in time. WannaCry attacked hundreds of thousands of computers. Banks, hospitals, and public transportation were just a few of the industries affected. The cyberattack caused major problems at hospitals in the United Kingdom. Medical records are usually stored on computers. Hospital workers could not access these records. Doctors had to reschedule thousands of medical procedures. Hospitals shut down emergency rooms.

British cybersecurity expert Marcus Hutchins helped stop the 2017 WannaCry attack.

YOU WOULDN'T
DOWNLOAD A ~~BEAR~~
↑
Fancy

ANONYMOUS CRIMINALS

Many cybercrimes go unnoticed or unreported. In some cases, people are not aware that they have been the victim of a cybercrime. Many people rely on security software to alert them to threats. But their software may not be up-to-date. Software that is outdated may not be able to detect new threats. In other cases, people may be embarrassed to admit they were victims of a cybercrime. Then they may not report the crime.

Some criminals would never try to rob someone in real life. But they steal from people online. This is because they can make themselves anonymous online. They can hide their real names and identities. They do this to keep people from finding out who they are. This makes it difficult for authorities to find cybercriminals.

STRAIGHT TO THE
SOURCE

In November 2018, the Marriott hotel chain's computer system was hacked. More than 500 million customer accounts were breached. Massachusetts senator Ed Markey remarked on the breach:

> *Checking in to a hotel should not mean checking out of privacy and security protections. Preventing massive data breaches isn't just about protecting privacy, it's also about protecting our pocketbooks. Breaches like this can lead to identity theft and crippling financial fraud. They are a black cloud hanging over the United States' bright economic horizon. The American people deserve real action. It's time for Congress to pass comprehensive consumer privacy and data security legislation that requires companies to adhere to strong data security standards.*

> Source: John Eggerton. "Marriot Breach Spurs New Calls for Government Action." *Multichannel News*. Multichannel News, November 30, 2018. Web. Accessed January 8, 2019.

Consider Your Audience

Adapt this passage for a different audience, such as your friends. Write a blog post conveying this same information for the new audience. How does your post differ from the original text and why?

STAYING SAFE

Technology is constantly changing. Today, many devices are connected to the internet. This network of interconnected devices is called the Internet of Things (IoT). Cybercriminals continue to develop new ways to hack into systems. Some find ways to hack into the IoT. Others use scams or software to hack into systems. Computer users can learn how to protect themselves from these cybercrimes.

NEW TYPES OF CRIME

The IoT has opened a new channel for cybercrimes. Hackers can find ways to take control of alarm systems and other IoT devices.

The Internet of Things includes smart devices, such as alarms that people can control from smartphone apps.

Some cybercriminals use bots to attack systems. A bot is a type of software. Bots perform specific tasks. Some bots gather information. They also answer questions through instant messaging. But other bots are bad. They can send spam. Spam includes messages meant to trick people into giving up information. Bots can also steal passwords and launch DoS attacks.

THE INTERNET OF THINGS

Some objects that have power switches can be connected to the internet. IoT devices can include watches, lamps, and fridges. People can monitor and control these devices remotely through the internet. For example, smart deadbolts on doors can be locked or unlocked using a mobile app. Experts think the IoT will have as many as 75 billion devices by 2025.

Cloning is another type of scam. It happens when a criminal gets the phone number and identifying information for a smartphone. The criminal programs another phone with the same information. Any charges for calls, texts, and data usage are sent to the original phone's owner.

In another common phone scam, criminals text people saying their bank account has been hacked. The text tells people to click on a website or reply to the text. When they do, malware is installed on their device. The malware collects their personal data. Criminals can use this data to steal their identity.

CYBERSECURITY

Some companies are working to protect themselves from cybercrimes. Many have developed policies and procedures to stop people from hacking into their systems. Some organizations hire white-hat hackers. White-hat hackers help find flaws in computer systems. Then companies can fix these flaws.

People can take steps to protect themselves from cybercrimes. Passwords can help secure accounts and devices. A strong password is long. It should have a mix of numbers and letters. It should also have special

Many smartphones scan users' fingerprints as an extra layer of security. The devices unlock when they recognize a fingerprint.

characters, such as symbols. People should never share their passwords. They should have a different password for each account or device. It is important to always log off of devices and accounts.

Another important security tool is multi-factor authentication (MFA). MFA can be used to protect data. It verifies that the person trying to access an account is the owner of the account. For example, people can use

MFA to protect their email accounts. They need to log in regularly. They also need to type in a code that is sent to their phone. In this way, MFA provides an extra layer of security.

People can also learn how to spot phishing scams. Many of these scams have typos or are poorly written. They may include offers that seem too good to be true. People should be wary of links and attachments in emails and texts. Even if

PERSPECTIVES
COPING WITH CRIME

Cybercrimes can be damaging in many ways. Some crimes are simply inconvenient. Others can cause emotional distress. Many victims face financial problems. Their reputation may be damaged. Or they may fear for their safety. Victims often feel like their personal space has been invaded. They may feel angry, guilty, or depressed. Some victims may find it hard to trust other people. They may try to avoid computers or the internet. Amy Krebs was the victim of identity theft. She felt as if someone had taken over her life. She said, "It's the most time-consuming, upsetting, emotional event you have to go through."

the email or text appears to be from a trusted source, it may be a phishing scam. Attachments in phishing scams could include malware. It is a good idea to check with the person or company that supposedly sent the message. People should also only download apps and software from trusted sites.

People should also update devices and software often. Updates often include patches that block bugs in the system. Hackers can take advantage of these bugs to break into a computer. Keeping antivirus software updated is important. Updated security software can defend a computer system against new threats.

Antivirus software scans show if a device is infected. If a device is infected, a computer expert may need to remove the threat or restore the computer's original settings. Victims should tell police about the crime. They may need to close accounts and cancel credit cards so they cannot be used. It is also a good idea to change the passwords for all accounts and devices.

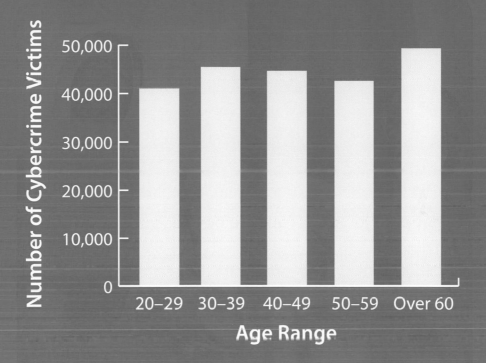

CYBERCRIME VICTIMS

Number of Cybercrime Victims (y-axis): 0, 10,000, 20,000, 30,000, 40,000, 50,000

Age Range (x-axis): 20–29, 30–39, 40–49, 50–59, Over 60

The above graph shows cybercrime victims in the United States by age group in 2017. Which age group seems to be most vulnerable to cybercrimes? Why do you think this is? How do you think people could address this problem?

Cybercrime is on the rise as more people use the internet. Technology is always changing. There may be new types of cybercrimes in the future. But there are many steps people can take to protect themselves from cybercrimes. Today, security experts and lawmakers continue to address cybercrime.

FAST FACTS

- Cybercrimes are crimes that happen through computers, computer networks, or devices connected to a network.

- Cybercrime is the fastest-growing type of crime in the United States. Identity theft, cyberstalking, and data breaches are some of the most common types of cybercrimes.

- Some hackers commit cybercrimes. They break into computer systems. They steal data for personal gain.

- Some hackers use malware to break into computer systems. Malware damages or destroys computers and systems. Ransomware is a type of malware that blocks access to files or encrypts them so they cannot be used until the victim pays a ransom.

- Many cybercriminals try to trick people into sharing personal information, such as passwords or credit card numbers.

- Being aware of common cybercrimes gives people a better chance at protecting themselves from an attack. People can also use passwords and security software to protect their devices.

STOP AND
THINK

Dig Deeper

After reading this book, what questions do you still have about cybercrime? With an adult's help, find a few reliable sources that can help you answer your questions. Write a paragraph about what you learned.

Why Do I Care?

Chapter Three describes how the invention of ARPANET paved the way for the modern internet. How does the internet affect your life today? How would your life be different if the internet had never been invented?

Surprise Me

Chapter Two discusses different types of cybercrimes. After reading this book, what two or three facts about cybercrimes did you find most surprising? Write a few sentences about each fact. Why did you find each fact surprising?

Tell the Tale

Chapter One discusses a ransomware attack that affected an entire city. Imagine that the city or town where you live was the victim of a ransomware attack. Write 200 words about how you think officials should respond to the attack. How do you think similar attacks could be avoided in the future?

GLOSSARY

anonymous
an unknown or unnamed person or group or people

app
a software program on a mobile device that has a specific purpose or function

breach
the act of breaking into something

bug
an error or flaw in a software program

code
a set of instructions that tell a computer what do to

encrypt
to make data unreadable

fraud
something designed to deceive others in return for financial gain

hacker
someone who breaks into computer systems

identity
the features that define who a person is

operating system
a type of software that controls a computer's main functions and runs other software

ONLINE RESOURCES

To learn more about cybercrime, visit our free resource websites below.

Visit **abdocorelibrary.com** or scan this QR code for free Common Core resources for teachers and students, including vetted activities, multimedia, and booklinks, for deeper subject comprehension.

Visit **abdobooklinks.com** or scan this QR code for free additional online weblinks for further learning. These links are routinely monitored and updated to provide the most current information available.

LEARN MORE

Rodger, Ellen. *Top Secret Science in Cybercrime and Espionage*. New York: Crabtree Publishing, 2019.

Smibert, Angie. *Inside Computers*. Minneapolis, MN: Abdo Publishing, 2019.

INDEX

About the Author

Heather C. Hudak has written hundreds of books for schools and libraries. When she is not writing, you can find her camping in the mountains with her husband and rescue pets or traveling the world. She loves eating pasta in Italy, visiting ancient temples in Indonesia, and searching for animals on the African savannah.